6
GCSE 9-1
Mathematics
Practice Papers

Higher Tier

Set A Paper 1

You must not use a calculator.

1)

Given that $a = \begin{pmatrix} 2 \\ 3 \end{pmatrix}$ and $b = \begin{pmatrix} -3 \\ 4 \end{pmatrix}$ find c such that $2a + c = 3b$.

$$2a = \begin{pmatrix} 4 \\ 6 \end{pmatrix} \qquad 3b = \begin{pmatrix} -9 \\ 12 \end{pmatrix}$$

$$2a - 3b = -c$$

$$\begin{pmatrix} 4 \\ 6 \end{pmatrix} - \begin{pmatrix} -9 \\ 12 \end{pmatrix} = \begin{pmatrix} 13 \\ -6 \end{pmatrix} \qquad \begin{pmatrix} 13 \\ -6 \end{pmatrix}$$

$\begin{pmatrix} 13 \\ -6 \end{pmatrix}$ .... (3)

✳ 2)

$\frac{8}{5}$ of $y = 96$.

Find the value of y.

$1\frac{3}{5}$ of $y = 96$

.... (2)

3)

Work out 3.5×64.7

$$\begin{array}{r} 64.7 \\ 3.5 \\ \hline 3235 \\ 19410 \\ \hline 226.45 \end{array}$$

....226.45.......... (3)

✳ 4)

$m = 2^3 \times 3 \times 5^2$ and $n = 2 \times 3^3 \times 5 \times 7$

Find the highest common factor and lowest common multiple of m and n.

Write your answers as products of prime factors.

$m = (2 \times 2 \times 2) \times 3 \times (5 \times 5)$

$m = 8 \times 3 \times 25$

$m = 75 \times 8 = 600$

$600 =$
$1890 =$

$n = 2 \times (3 \times 3 \times 3) \times 5 \times 7$

$n = 2 \times 27 \times 35$

$n = 54 \times 35 = 1890$

$$\begin{array}{r} 75 \\ \times 8 \\ \hline 600 \end{array}$$

$$\begin{array}{r} 54 \\ \times 35 \\ \hline 270 \\ 1620 \\ \hline 1890 \end{array}$$

Highest common factor .... (1)

Lowest Common multiple .... (1)

5)

✳ Factorise $4x^2 - 3x - 10$.

F $4x^2$
$-8x$
$5x$
-10

.... (2)

6)

The mean salary of the three directors of a company is £100 000.
The company employs 203 people including the directors. The mean salary of all 203
employees is £30 000. What is the mean salary of the employees who are not directors?

.... (3)

7)

Make u the subject of the formula

$$v^2 = u^2 + 2as$$

.... (2)

8)

Show that $0.07\dot{8} = \frac{13}{165}$

(2)

9)

The sets A and B are defined below.
$A = \{2,4,6,810,12\}$
$B = \{1,2,3,4,5\}$

a) Find $n(A \cup B)$

.... (2)

b) Find $n(A \cap B)$

.... (2)

10)

Estimate the value of $\dfrac{304.7 \times 68.9}{0.298}$

.... (2)

11)

a) Find the value of $27^{-\frac{1}{3}}$

.... (2)

b) Find the value of $\left(\dfrac{25}{36}\right)^{\frac{3}{2}}$

.... (2)

12)

Solve the simultaneous equations

$$x^2 + y^2 = 13$$
$$2x - y = 8$$

.... (5)

13)

A straight line passes through the points $(2,3)$ and $(4,6)$.

Another straight line has equation $2x + 3y = 5$.

Show that the lines are perpendicular.

(3)

14)

The diagram below shows a circle and a tangent.

The tangent touches the circle at the point (4,6).

Find the area shaded in the diagram, giving your answer in the form
$\frac{a}{b} - c\pi$, where a, b and c are integers.

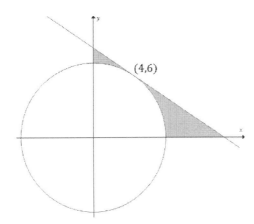

.... (6)

15)

Work out $\sqrt[6]{6.4 \times 10^{13}}$.

.... (3)

16)

ABCD is a parallelogram.

Prove that triangle ADE is congruent to triangle CBE.

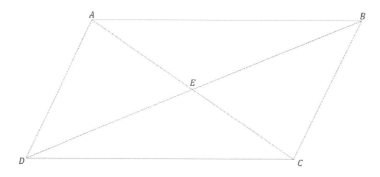

.... (4)

17)

Simplify $\frac{12}{\sqrt{2}} + 7\sqrt{8}$ giving your answer in the form $a\sqrt{2}$ where a is an integer.

.... (3)

18)

A flask holds 5 litres of water in which 15 grams of salt is dissolved.

Another container holds a solution with a concentration of 20 grams of salt per litre of water. How much of the second solution must be added to the first solution to increase the concentration to 4 grams per litre?

.... (5)

19)

$ABDE$ is a parallelogram.
$\overrightarrow{AB} = \boldsymbol{p}$
$\overrightarrow{AF} = 3\boldsymbol{q}$
The ratio of BC to CD is 1:3 and the ratio of AF to FE is 3:1.

Express $\overrightarrow{AG}$ in terms $\boldsymbol{p}$ and $\boldsymbol{q}$.

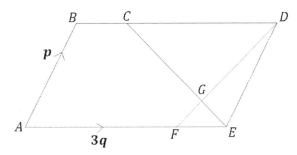

.... (4)

20)

There are 16 discs in a box. Some of them are blue and some are green. There are more blue discs than green discs. Two discs are taken, at random, from the box. The first disc is not replaced in the box. The probability that one disc of each colour is taken is $\frac{21}{40}$.

Find the number of blue discs and the number of green discs in the box.

.... (4)

21)

Given that BD bisects angle ABC, calculate the length of BD.

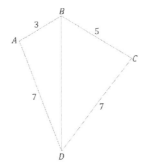

.... (4)

22)

Given that y is inversely proportional to x and that $y = 9$ when $x = 4$,
find the possible values of x if $x + y = 20$.

.... (4)

23)

The diagram below shows a circle with perpendicular diameters which are tangents to the
smaller circle. The two circles are mutually tangent. What is the ratio of the area of the
smaller circle to the area of the larger circle? Give your answer in its exact form.

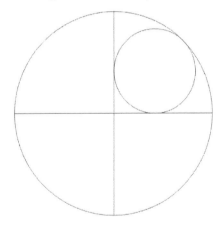

.... (6)

Set A Paper 2

You may use a calculator.

1)
    a) Write 376500000 in standard form.

                                                    .... (1)

    b) Write 0.00000465 in standard form.

                                                    .... (1)

2)

19 students got the following marks in a maths test.

32, 35, 43, 44, 48, 56, 57, 58, 59, 62,
63, 67, 70, 74, 77, 80, 80, 80, 80

Draw a box plot for this information.

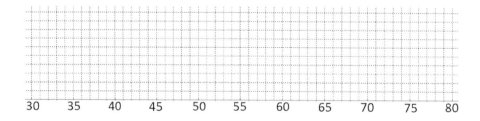

(3)

3)

Use your calculator to workout $\dfrac{1.2^3 - \sqrt{2.3^2 - 1.09^2}}{\sqrt[3]{5.7}}$.

a) Write down all the figures on your calculator display.

.... (2)

b) Give your answer to three significant figures.

.... (1)

4)

The first five numbers in a Fibonacci type sequence are

$3, x, 10, y, z$

Write down the values of x, y and z.

.... (2)

5)

Find the size of angle ABC.

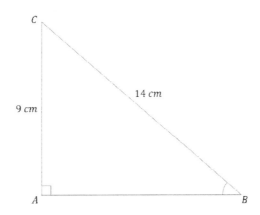

.... (2)

6)

Factorise $x^2 - 2x - 15$

.... (2)

7)

Change 6.3 cm³ to mm³.

.... (2)

8)

Describe fully the single transformation that maps shape A onto shape B.

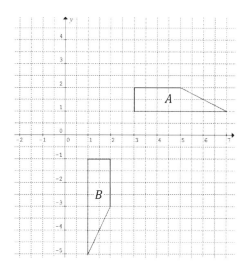

....
.... (3)

9)

Expand and simplify $4(x - 3) + 6(4x + 6)$

.... (2)

10)

Simplify $4a^2b^3 \times 3ab^4$

 (2)

11)

The diagram shows two regular hexadecagons. They each have 16 sides. Find the size of the angle marked x.

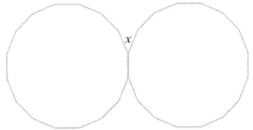

.... (4)

12)

In a school the ratio of teachers to pupils is 1:7 and the ratio of boys to girls is 6:8.

If there are 120 more girls than boys in the school, how many teachers are there?

.... (4)

13)

The price of a coat is reduced by 15% in a sale. If the price is reduced by £38.25, what was the price of the coat before the sale?

.... (2)

14)

The diagram below shows a sector of a circle.

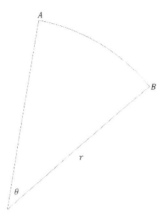

The length of the arc AB is 2π cm and the area of the sector is 9π cm^2.
Write down two equations and solve them to find r and θ.

.... (6)

15)

Work out the exact value of $2.73 \times 10^{104} \times 5.77 \times 10^{87}$ giving your answer in standard form.

.... (2)

16)

Solve $3(x + 5) = \frac{2x-4}{4}$

.... (2)

17)

Solve $3x^2 - 7x = 13$

Give your answers correct to three significant figures.

.... (4)

18)

$f(x) = x^2 + 1$ $g(x) = x - 7$

Show that $fg(x) = x^2 - 14x + 50$.

Find $gf(x)$.

.... (4)

Solve $fg(x) = gf(x)$.

.... (4)

19)

How many four digit numbers are there for which the first digit is odd and the second digit is prime?

.... (2)

20)

Find the exact area of quadrilateral $ABCD$. Write your answer in the form $\frac{a}{b}\left(\sqrt{c}+\sqrt{d}\right)$ where a, b, c and d are integers.

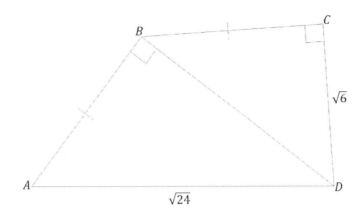

.... (5)

21)

Show that $\left(2+\sqrt{2}\right)\left(1-\sqrt{2}\right)\left(3-\sqrt{2}\right) = 2 - 3\sqrt{2}$

(4)

22)

The graph of $y = f(x)$ has a minimum point at (8,2).

Write down the coordinates of the minimum point on the graph of $y = 3f(2x)$.

.... (2)

23)

The diagram shows a circle, centre O. Points A, B and C lie on the circle. AD is a tangent to the circle at A.

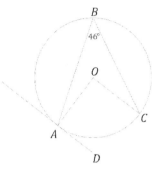

B

46°

O

C

A

D

Find the size of angles AOC and CAD, giving reasons for your answers.

Angle AOC ....

....

.... (2)

Angle CAD ....

....

.... (2)

24)

A fish farmer captured 30 fish from her lake and marked them. She then released them and later captured 50 fish. Of those 50 fish, 17 were found to be marked. Calculate an estimate of the number of fish in the lake.

.... (4)

25)

The first three terms of a quadratic sequence are 2, 9 and 20.

Find an expression for the nth term of the sequence.

.... (4)

Set A Paper 3
You may use a calculator.

1)

$x = 3.65$ correct to two decimal places. Write the error interval for x.

.... (1)

$y = 2.7$ truncated to two decimal places. Write the error interval for y.

.... (1)

2)

A circle has a radius of 15 cm. Calculate the area of the circle giving you answer correct to 3 significant figures.

.... (2)

3)

The first two terms of a geometric sequence are $2\sqrt{5}$ and $10\sqrt{3}$.
What is the next term?

.... (3)

4)

After a 5% pay rise, Bob earns £9.03 per hour. What was his hourly rate before the pay rise?

.... (3)

5)

The diagrams below show three views of an object. Make a sketch of a three-dimensional view of the object.

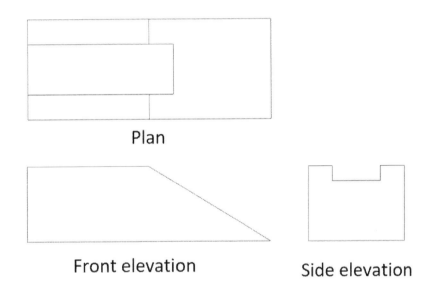

Plan

Front elevation

Side elevation

(3)

6)

Solve the equation $1.05^3 \times x^4 = 1.3$.

.... (2)

7)

Given that $2x + 6y = 19$ and $3x - 4y = 9$ solve the simultaneous equations to show that $x = 5$ and $y = \frac{3}{2}$

(4)

8)

Estimate the interquartile range for the data summarised in the histogram below.

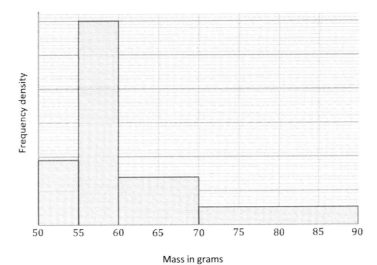

Mass in grams

.... (5)

9)

Simplify $\dfrac{3x^2-48}{5x-15} \div \dfrac{3x+12}{25}$

.... (4)

10)

A ship sails 60km on a bearing on 060°. It then turns and sails 100km on a bearing of 170°.
Calculate its distance from its starting point.
Calculate the bearing it would have to sail on to return to its starting point.

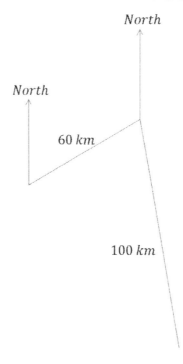

Distance .... (3)

Bearing .... (3)

11)

Write $3x^2 - 12x + 2$ in the form $a(x + b)^2 + c$.

.... (3)

12)

The table below shows the masses of some eggs.

Mass, m grams	Frequency
$40 \leq m < 45$	3
$45 \leq m < 50$	6
$50 \leq m < 55$	12
$55 \leq m < 60$	4
$60 \leq m < 65$	3

a) Calculate an estimate of the mean mass of the eggs.

.... (3)

b) Work out which interval the median lies in.

.... (2)

13)

Write down three inequalities that define the region labelled R, below.

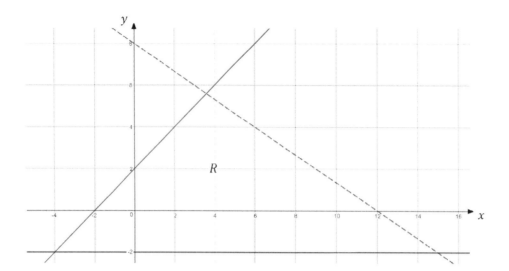

....

....

.... (3)

14)

A cuboid has edges with lengths 5cm, 12cm and 84cm. Find the greatest distance between vertices of the cuboid.

.... (5)

15)

Construct an angle of 30°.

(4)

16)

Here are some facts about the Earth and the moon. Assuming the Earth and the moon to be mathematically similar, work out the mass of the moon, in kilograms, giving your answer in standard form.

	Density	Radius	Mass
Earth	5520 kg/m^3	6371 km	5.97 $\times$ 10^{24} kg
Moon	3340 kg/m^3	1737 km	

.... (4)

17)

Show that the equation $x^2 - 9x - 3 = 0$ can be rearranged to give $x = \frac{3+9x}{x}$.

(2)

Use the iterative formula $x_{n+1} = \frac{3+9x_n}{x_n}$ with a starting value of $x_1 = 8$ to find a solution of the quadratic equation correct to two decimal places.

.... (3)

18)

The first three terms of an arithmetic sequence are 9, 17 and 25.

Prove that the difference between the squares of **any** two terms in the sequence is divisible by 16.

(5)

19)

Solve the inequality $2x^2 - 5x - 3 < 0$.

.... (3)

20)

The value of V correct to two significant figures is 6.1.

The value of R correct to two significant figures is 1.8.

$$P = \frac{V^2}{R}$$

Find the value of P to an appropriate degree of accuracy.

.... (5)

21)
The diagram below shows a circle, centre O.

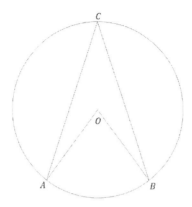

Prove that angle AOB is twice angle ACB.

(4)

Set B Paper 1
You must not use a calculator.

1)

Work out 3.6×0.009

................................(2)

2)

Simplify $\dfrac{(3x^2 \times 4x^2)^2}{6x^2}$

................................(3)

3)

Work out an estimate for $\dfrac{18.12 \times 307.64}{59.7}$

................................(3)

4)

(a) Round 6478700 to three significant figures.

................................(1)

(b) Round 0.0009762087 to three significant figures.

................................(1)

5)

Given that $x = -0.9$ write the following numbers in ascending order.

$$x^{-1} \qquad x^2 \qquad x^3 \qquad x^0$$

.... (2)

6)

$x = 0.6\dot{2}\dot{1}.$

Prove algebraically that $x = \frac{41}{66}$

.... (2)

7)

Describe fully the single transformation that maps triangle A onto triangle B.

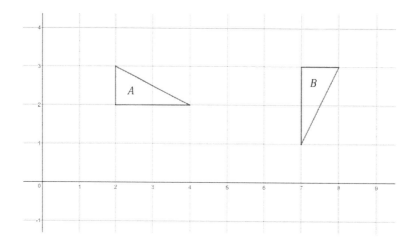

.... (2)

8)

Work out $4\frac{1}{5} \times 1\frac{2}{7}$ giving your answer as a mixed number in its simplest form.

.... (2)

9)

Find the exact value of $\cos 45° \times \tan 30° + \sin 45° \times \tan 60°$

giving your answer in the form $\frac{a\sqrt{b}}{c}$.

.... (4)

10)

(a) Write down the equation of a line that is parallel to the line with equation $2x + 3y = 5$.

..........................(1)

(b) Find an equation of the line that passes through the point $(-2,3)$ and is perpendicular to the line with equation $2x + 3y = 5$.

..........................(1)

11)

Bob thinks that x^2 is always greater than x.

(a) Solve the inequality $x^2 > x$ to find the interval for which Bob's belief is wrong.

 (2)

(b) Sketch graphs on the grid below showing the straight line with equation $y = x$ and the curve with equation $y = x^2$ and explain how your sketch relates to part (a).

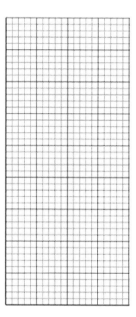

.... (3)

12)

$x = \dfrac{2^a}{2^b}$ and a and b are integers.

What is the relationship between a and b in each of the following cases?

(a) x is not an integer.

...........................(1)

(b) x is an odd number.

...........................(1)

(c) x is an even number.

...........................(1)

13)

Is the point (3,7) inside or outside the circle with equation $x^2 + y^2 = 60$?

.... (2)

14)

Mary and Bob are painting one side a wall. The wall is 6m long and 1.5m high. If Mary paints $1m^2$ every eight minutes and Bob paints $1m^2$ every ten minutes how long will they take to finish painting the wall?

.... (3)

15)

The scatter graph below shows the results from eight experiments. Estimate the volume of hydrogen that would be produced after six minutes.

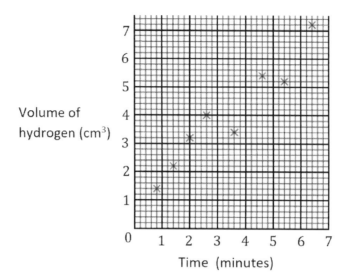

Volume of hydrogen (cm³)

Time (minutes)

.... (2)

16)

Expand and simplify $\frac{(2x+2)(3x-4)}{x}$ writing your answer in the form $ax + b + cx^d$, where a, b, c and d are integers.

.... (3)

17)

Simplify $\dfrac{1}{1-\frac{1}{\sqrt{3}}}$

.... (3)

18)

Calculate the area of the triangle below giving your answer in the form $a\sqrt{b}$, where a and b are integers.

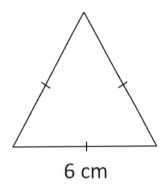

6 cm

.... (4)

19)

The heights of 32 adults are summarised in the table below.

Height, h (metres)	Frequency
$1.5 \leq h < 1.6$	3
$1.6 \leq h < 1.7$	5
$1.7 \leq h < 1.8$	10
$1.8 \leq h < 1.9$	12
$1.9 \leq h < 2.0$	2

(a) On the grid, plot a cumulative frequency graph for this information.

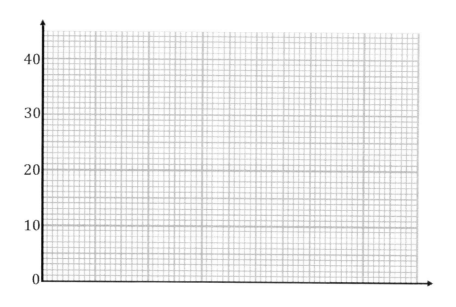

.... (2)

(b) Use your graph to find an estimate of the interquartile range of the heights.

.... (2)

(c) What is the probability that a randomly chosen adult from this group will be less than 1.7m tall?

.... (1)

20)

Solve $\frac{1}{x} = x - \frac{8}{x}$

.... (3)

21)

The first three terms of a quadratic sequence are 4, 12 and 24.

Find an expression for the nth term of the sequence.

.... (4)

22)

Simplify $\dfrac{6x^2-3x-3}{12x^2+14x+4}$

.... (4)

23)

A triangle has sides $AB = 5$cm, $BC = 7$cm and $AC = 8$cm. Find the size of angle BAC.

.... (6)

24)

Solve the simultaneous equations

$$x^2 + y^2 = 10$$
$$x + 2y = 5$$

.... (5)

25)

Use the graph of $y = f(x)$ below to find the value of $ff(2)$.

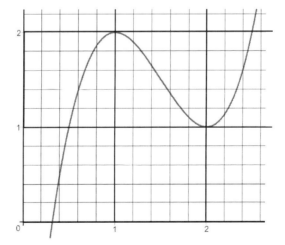

.... (2)

Write down the value of $fffff(2)$.

.... (2)

Set B Paper 2

You may use a calculator.

1)

Use your calculator to work out $\dfrac{\sqrt{2.3^3+1.1\times9.3}+4.6}{2.07^3\times4.871}$

.... (2)

2)

The first term of a Fibonacci type sequence is 2 and the sixth term is 41. What is the third term of the sequence?

.... (2)

3)

ABC is a right-angled triangle. Work out the size of angle CBA. Give your answer correct to the nearest degree.

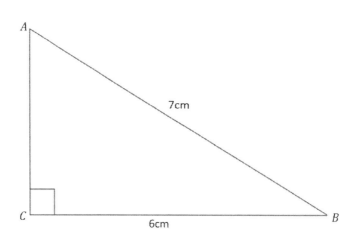

.... (2)

4)

Solve $x^2 - 9x - 7 = 0$ giving your solutions correct to three significant figures.

.... (3)

5)

A box, in the shape of a cuboid, has length 100cm, width 70cm and height 50cm.

A standard size football has a radius of 11.5cm.

Show that it is possible to fit 24 of these balls in the box and that it is not possible to fit 55 of these balls in the box.

(4)

6)

Expand and simplify $(2x + 3)(3x - 2) - 4(x - 5)$

.... (3)

7) The area of the triangle below is 8cm². The sides of the triangle are tangents to the circle. Find the area that is shaded.

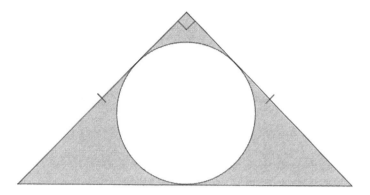

.... (5)

8)

The functions f and g are defined such that $f(x) = x + 3$ and $g(x) = x - 5$.
Solve the equation $f(x)g(x) = 20$.

.... (4)

9)

Make x the subject of the formula $y = ax + bx$.

....(2)

10)

Solve the simultaneous equations

$$4x - 2y = 7$$
$$6x + 6y = 24$$

$x=$.......................................

$y=$.......................................

(4)

11)

The table below gives information about the times taken by 24 athletes to run 100m.

Time (t seconds)	Frequency
$9.9 \leq t < 10.1$	3
$10.1 \leq t < 10.3$	6
$10.3 \leq t < 10.35$	9
$10.35 \leq t < 10.4$	4
$10.4 \leq t < 10.6$	2

(a) On the grid draw a histogram for the information in the table.

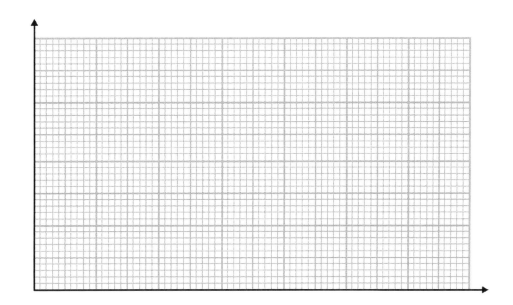

(3)

(b) Estimate the number of athletes who have times below 10.2 seconds.

....(1)

12)

Solve $3(x - 5) = 6(2x + 4)$

....(2)

13)

A block of ice measures 12cm by 10cm by 5cm. The ice is melted and transferred to a cylindrical container. The diameter of the container is 15cm. The density of ice is 0.92 g/cm^3. The density of water is 1 g/cm^3. Calculate the depth of water in the container.

....(6)

14)

The first term of an arithmetic sequence is 7 and the sum of the first four terms is 37. Find an expression for the nth term of the sequence.

....(6)

15)

An arithmetic sequence starts with the terms 7,13,19,25. Prove that the difference between the squares of any two consecutive terms is a multiple of 24.

....(5)

16)

The difference between two consecutive cubes is 22447. What are the two cubes?

....(6)

17)

Amy, Bob and Carol share some money in the ratio 7:5:4. Between them Amy and Carol receive £180 more than Bob. How much does Bob get?

....(3)

18)

Bob invested £2000 in a bank account for four years. The account paid compound interest. At the end of four years Bob had £2251.05 in his account. What was the interest rate?

....(3)

19)

Triangle ABC has sides $AB = 9$ cm, $BC = 5$ cm and angle $BAC = 26°$.

(a) Use a ruler, protractor and compasses to make accurate drawings of the two possible triangles which satisfy these requirements.

....(4)

(b)

Calculate the two possible values for angle BCA.

....(3)

20)
The diagram below shows a circle and a square. The radius of the circle is 2cm.
Calculate the area of the square.

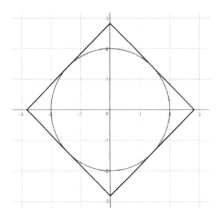

....(1)

21)

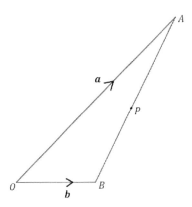

If the ratio $AP:PB$ is $x:y$ show that the $\overrightarrow{OP} = \frac{1}{x+y}(y\boldsymbol{a} + x\boldsymbol{b})$

....(6)

Set B Paper 3

You may use a calculator.

1)

(a) Calculate the area of the trapezium shown below.

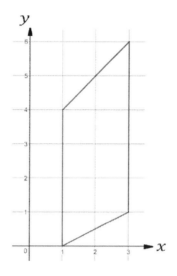

....(2)

(b) Calculate the perimeter of the trapezium.

....(3)

2)

Simplify

(a) $\frac{1}{4^{-2}}$

....(1)

(b) $(6x^3y^2)^0$

....(1)

3)

Expand and simplify $(4x - 3)(2x + 5)$.

....(2)

4)

Simplify $\frac{12x^3y}{2xy^4}$

....(2)

5)

Given that $a \neq 0$ and $b \neq 0$ show that the lines with equations $ax + by = c$ and $bx - ay = d$ are perpendicular.

....(5)

6)

Prove algebraically that $(3n + 1)^2 - (3n + 1)$ is a multiple of 3 for all positive integer values of n.

....(3)

7)

Given that $a = 2 + \sqrt{3}$ and $b = 2 - \sqrt{3}$, simplify each expression below.

(a) $a + b$

....(1)

(b) ab

....(2)

(c) $\frac{a}{b}$

....(2)

8)

Factorise completely $ax^2 + bx^2 - axy - bxy$.

....(2)

9) Write as a single fraction

(a) $2 - \dfrac{2x}{x+2}$

....(2)

(b) $\dfrac{2}{x+4} + \dfrac{2}{x^2+7x+12}$

....(4)

10) Show that the equation $x^3 + 2x - 26 = 0$ can be rearranged to give $x = \sqrt[3]{26 - 2x}$.

Use the iterative formula $x_{n+1} = \sqrt[3]{26 - 2x_n}$, with a starting value of $x_0 = 3$ to find a solution of the equation giving your answer correct to 3 decimal places.

....(5)

11) Solve $3^a \times 5^3 = 45 \times 225$

....(2)

12)

(a) Factorise $9x^2 - 1$

....(2)

(b) Factorise $9x^4 - 1$

....(2)

13)

By referring to an appropriate diagram, show that $\cos 30° = \frac{\sqrt{3}}{2}$.

....(4)

14)

(a) Factorise the expression $3x^2 - 8x + 4$

....(2)

(b) Solve the equation $3x^2 - 8x + 4 = 0$

....(1)

15)

Make x the subject of the formula $k = \dfrac{m(2+x)}{7-x}$

....(4)

16)

Complete the table below and plot the graph of $y = 2 + 3x - x^2$.

x	-1	0	1	2	3	4
y						

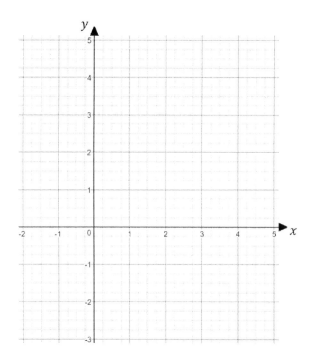

(3)

17)

The functions f and g are defined below.

$f(x) = x - 3$ $\qquad$ $g(x) = x^2 + 1$

(a) Find $g(x + 1)$, giving your answer in its simplest form.

 ....(2)

(b) Find $gf(x)$.

 ....(2)

(c) Find $f^{-1}(3)$

 ....(2)

18)

The line with equation $x + 2y = 10$ crosses the x axis at A.
The line with equation $y = x + 2$ crosses the x axis at B.
The lines intersect at P.
Find the area of triangle ABP.

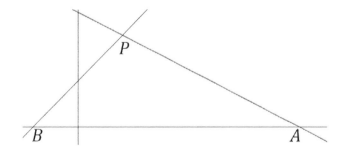

....(5)

19)

$a = 4.53 \times 10^{87}$

$b = 2.76 \times 10^{-37}$

$c = \dfrac{a}{b^2}$

Calculate the value of c giving your answer in standard form, correct to three significant figures.

....(5)

20)

There are n red beads and 7 blue beads in a box. Bob takes, at random, two beads from the box. The probability that Bob takes one bead of each colour is $\frac{8}{15}$.

Show that $4n^2 - 53n + 168 = 0$.

....(4)

Find the probability that Bob takes two blue beads.

....(3)

1)

$$c = 3b - 2a = \begin{pmatrix} -9 \\ 12 \end{pmatrix} - \begin{pmatrix} 4 \\ 6 \end{pmatrix} = \begin{pmatrix} -13 \\ 6 \end{pmatrix}$$

2)

$$\frac{8y}{5} = 96 \Rightarrow y = \frac{96 \times 5}{8} = 12 \times 5 = 60$$

3)

$$3.5 \times 64.7 = 226.45$$

4)

HCF $= 2 \times 3 \times 5$ LCM $= 2^3 \times 3^3 \times 5^2 \times 7$

5)

$$4x^2 - 3x - 10 \equiv (4x + 5)(x - 2)$$

6)

$$\frac{203 \times 30000 - 3 \times 100000}{200} = \frac{6090000 - 300000}{200} = \frac{579000}{200} = 28950$$

7)

$$v^2 - 2as = u^2 \Rightarrow u = \sqrt{v^2 - 2as}$$

8)

Let $x = 0.0\dot{7}\dot{8}$
$10x = 0.\dot{7}\dot{8}$
$1000x = 78.\dot{7}\dot{8}$
$990x = 78$
$x = \frac{78}{990} = \frac{13}{165}$

9)

$A \cup B = \{1,2,3,4,5,6,810,12\}$
$n(A \cup B) = 9$
$A \cap B = \{2,4\}$
$n(A \cap B) = 2$

10)

$$\frac{304.7 \times 68.9}{0.298} \approx \frac{300 \times 70}{0.3} = \frac{3000}{3} \times 70 = 70000$$

11)

$$27^{-\frac{1}{3}} = \frac{1}{\sqrt[3]{27}} = \frac{1}{3}$$
$$\left(\frac{25}{36}\right)^{\frac{3}{2}} = \left(\frac{\sqrt{25}}{\sqrt{36}}\right)^3 = \left(\frac{5}{6}\right)^3 = \frac{125}{216}$$

12)

$2x - y = 8 \Rightarrow y = 2x - 8 \Rightarrow y^2 = 4x^2 - 32x + 64$

$x^2 + 4x^2 - 32x + 64 = 13 \Rightarrow 5x^2 - 32x + 51 = 0 \Rightarrow (5x - 17)(x - 3) = 0$

$\Rightarrow x = \dfrac{17}{5}$ or $x = 3$

If $x = \dfrac{17}{5}$ then $y = 2 \times \dfrac{17}{5} - \dfrac{40}{5} = -\dfrac{6}{5}$

If $x = 3$ then $y = 2 \times 3 - 8 = -2$

$x = 3$ and $y = -2$ or $x = \dfrac{17}{5}$ and $y = -\dfrac{6}{5}$

13)

The gradient of the first line is $\dfrac{6-3}{4-2} = \dfrac{3}{2}$

For the second line $2x + 3y = 5 \Rightarrow 3y = -2x + 5 \Rightarrow y = -\dfrac{2}{3}x + \dfrac{5}{3}$

The gradient of the second line is $-\dfrac{2}{3}$.

The product of the gradients of the lines is $\dfrac{3}{2} \times -\dfrac{2}{3} = -1$ therefore the lines are perpendicular.

14)

The gradient of the radius to (4,6) is $\dfrac{6}{4} = \dfrac{3}{2}$ so the gradient of the tangent is $-\dfrac{2}{3}$.

The tangent has equation $y = -\dfrac{2}{3}x + c$ and passes through (4,6).

$c = y + \dfrac{2}{3}x = 6 + \dfrac{2}{3} \times 4 = \dfrac{6}{1} + \dfrac{8}{3} = \dfrac{18}{3} + \dfrac{8}{3} = \dfrac{26}{3}$

The equation of the tangent is $y = -\dfrac{2}{3}x + \dfrac{26}{3}$.

On the line, when $x = 0$, $y = \dfrac{26}{3}$.

When $y = 0, \dfrac{2}{3}x = \dfrac{26}{3} \Rightarrow 2x = 26 \Rightarrow x = 13$.

The triangle has a base of 13 and a height of $\dfrac{26}{3}$.

Its area is therefore $\dfrac{1}{2} \times 13 \times \dfrac{26}{3} = \dfrac{169}{3}$.

The equation of the circle is $x^2 + y^2 = r^2$ where $r^2 = 4^2 + 6^2 = 52$.

The area of the $\dfrac{1}{4}$ circle is therefore $\dfrac{52\pi}{4} = 13\pi$ and the shaded area is $\dfrac{169}{3} - 13\pi$.

15)

$\sqrt[6]{6.4 \times 10^{13}} = \sqrt[6]{64 \times 10^{12}} = \sqrt[6]{64} \times (10^{12})^{\frac{1}{6}} = 2 \times 10^2 = 200$

16)

Angle DAC = angle ACB. Alternate angles are equal.

Angle ADB = angle DCB. Alternate angles are equal.

$AD = BC$. Opposite sides of a parallelogram are equal.

Triangles ADE and CBE are congruent by SAS.

17)

$\dfrac{12}{\sqrt{2}} + 7\sqrt{8} = \dfrac{12\sqrt{2}}{2} + 7 \times 2\sqrt{2} = 6\sqrt{2} + 14\sqrt{2} = 20\sqrt{2}$

18)

Let the quantity required be x.

x litres with a concentration of 20g/l holds $20x$ grams of salt.

The original flask now holds $(5 + x)$ litres of water and $(15 + 20x)$ grams of salt.

It is required that $\frac{15+20x}{5+x} = 4$.

$\frac{15+20x}{5+x} = 4 \Rightarrow 15 + 20x = 20 + 4x \Rightarrow 16x = 5 \Rightarrow x = \frac{5}{16}\, l.$

19)

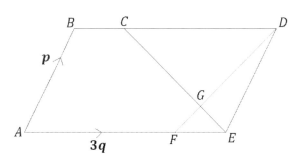

Triangles FGE and DGC are similar and $CD = 3FE$ therefore $FG = \frac{1}{4}FD$.

$$\overrightarrow{AG} = \overrightarrow{AF} + \overrightarrow{FG} = 3q + \frac{1}{4}\overrightarrow{FD} = 3q + \frac{1}{4}(q + p) = \frac{1}{4}p + \left(3 + \frac{1}{4}\right)q = \frac{1}{4}(p + 13q)$$

20)

Let the number of blue discs be b. The number of green discs is then $16 - b$.

$P(B, G) = \frac{b}{16} \times \frac{16-b}{15}$
$P(G, B) = P(B, G)$

$2 \times \frac{b}{16} \times \frac{16-b}{15} = \frac{21}{40} \Rightarrow 16b - b^2 = \frac{21 \times 16 \times 15}{40 \times 2} = 63$

$b^2 - 16b + 63 = 0 \Rightarrow (b - 7)(b - 9) = 0$

There are 9 blue discs and 7 green discs.

21)

Let $BD = x$.

By the cosine rule

$\frac{3^2 + x^2 - 7^2}{2 \times 3 \times x} = \frac{5^2 + x^2 - 7^2}{2 \times 5 \times x} \Rightarrow$

$5(x^2 - 40) = 3(x^2 - 24) \Rightarrow 2x^2 = 128 \Rightarrow x^2 = 64 \Rightarrow x = 8.$

22)

$$y = \frac{36}{x}$$

$$x + \frac{36}{x} = 20 \Rightarrow x^2 - 20x + 36 = 0 \Rightarrow (x - 2)(x - 18) = 0$$

$x = 2$ or $x = 18$.

23)

Let the radius of the larger circle be 1 and the radius of the smaller circle be r.

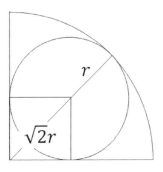

As shown in the diagram $r + \sqrt{2}r = 1$.

$$r\left(1 + \sqrt{2}\right) = 1 \Rightarrow r = \frac{1}{1+\sqrt{2}} = \sqrt{2} - 1 \text{ and } r^2 = 3 - 2\sqrt{2}.$$

The area of the smaller circle is $\left(3 - 2\sqrt{2}\right)\pi$.
The area of the larger circle is π.

The required ratio is $3 - 2\sqrt{2} : 1$
You might also arrive at the answer $1 : 3 + 2\sqrt{2}$. The two answers are equivalent.

1)

   a) 3.765×10^8

   b) 4.65×10^{-6}

2)

Minimum value = 32

$\frac{19}{4} = 4.75$. The lower quartile is the 5th number. Lower quartile = 48.

$\frac{19}{2} = 9.5$ the median is the 10th number. Median = 62.

$\frac{3 \times 19}{4} = 14.25$. The lower quartile is the 15th number. Upper quartile = 77.

Maximum value = 80.

3)

-0.1664402001

-0.166

4)

$x = 10 - 3 = 7, \ y = 17 + 10 = 17, z = 10 + 17 = 27$

5)

$\sin ABC = \frac{9}{14} \Rightarrow ABC = \sin^{-1} \frac{9}{14} \Rightarrow ABC = 40°$

6)

$(x - 4)(x + 3)$

7)

1 cm^3 =(1 cm)^3 =(10 mm)^3 = 1000 mm^3.

6.3cm^3 = 6300 mm^3

8)

Rotation 90° clockwise about the point (1,1).

9)

$4(x - 3) + 6(4x + 6) = 4x - 12 + 24x + 36 = 28x + 24$

10)

$4a^2b^3 \times 3ab^4 = 12a^3b^7$

11)

The exterior angle of a regular hexadecagon = $\frac{360}{16} = 22.5°$

$x = 2 \times 22.5°$

$x = 45°$

12)

$8 - 6 = 2$

$120 \div 2 = 60$

$60 \times (8 + 6) = 840$

$840 \div 7 = 120$

There are 120 teachers.

13)

$$\frac{\theta}{360°} \times 2\pi r = 2\pi \qquad \Rightarrow \qquad \theta r = 360° \qquad (1)$$

$$\frac{\theta}{360°} \times \pi r^2 = 9\pi \qquad \Rightarrow \qquad \theta r^2 = 9 \times 360° \qquad (2)$$

Dividing equation (2) by equation (1) gives $r = 9$cm.

Substituting in (1) gives $9\theta = 360°$ so $\theta = 40°$

14)

$0.15 \times$ original price = £38.25 $\Rightarrow$ original price $= \frac{£38.25}{0.15} = £255$.

15)

$$2.73 \times 10^{104} \times 5.77 \times 10^{87} = 2.73 \times 5.77 \times 10^{104+87} = 15.7521 \times 10^{191}.$$

16)

$3(x + 5) = \frac{2x-4}{4} \Rightarrow 3x + 15 = \frac{2x-4}{4} \Rightarrow$
$12x + 60 = 2x - 4 \Rightarrow 10x = -64 \Rightarrow x = -6.4$

17)

$3x^2 - 7x = 13 \Rightarrow 3x^2 - 7x - 13 = 0$

Using the quadratic formula with $a = 3, b = -7$ and $c = -13$

$$x = \frac{7 \pm \sqrt{(-7)^2 - 4 \times 3 \times -13}}{2 \times 3}$$

$$x = \frac{7 \pm \sqrt{205}}{6}$$

Correct to 3 significant figures $x = 3.55$ or $x = -1.22$

18)

$$fg(x) = f(x - 7) = (x - 7)^2 + 1 = x^2 - 14x + 49 + 1 = x^2 - 14x + 50$$

$$gf(x) = g(x^2 + 1) = x^2 + 1 - 7 = x^2 - 6$$

$$fg(x) = g(f(x) = x^2 - 14x + 50 = x^2 - 6 \Rightarrow 14x = 56 \Rightarrow x = 4$$

19)

The number of possible values for each of the digits is 5, 4, 10 and 10.

The number of possible numbers is $5 \times 4 \times 10 \times 10 = 2000$.

20)

Let $BC = x$.

By Pythagoras' theorem applied to both triangles

$x^2 + 6 = BD^2$ and $x^2 + BD^2 = 24$

$2x^2 + 6 = 24 \Rightarrow 2x^2 = 18 \Rightarrow x^2 = 9 \Rightarrow x = 3.$

$BD = \sqrt{9 + 6} = \sqrt{15}$

Total area = $\dfrac{3\sqrt{15} + 3\sqrt{6}}{2} = \dfrac{3}{2}\left(\sqrt{15} + \sqrt{6}\right)$

21)

$(2 + \sqrt{2})(1 - \sqrt{2})(3 - \sqrt{2}) = (2 + \sqrt{2})(3 - \sqrt{2} - 3\sqrt{2} + 2)$
$= (2 + \sqrt{2})(5 - 4\sqrt{2}) = 10 - 8\sqrt{2} + 5\sqrt{2} - 8 = 2 - 3\sqrt{2}$

22)

(4,6)

23)

$AOC = 92°$ The angle at the centre is twice the angle at the circumference.

$CAD = 46°$ Alternate segment theorem.

24)

Let the estimated number of fish be x.

From the second sample you can see that approximately $\dfrac{17}{50}$ of the fish are marked.

Therefore $30 = \dfrac{17}{50}x$.

$\dfrac{17}{50}x = 30 \Rightarrow 17x = 30 \times 50 \Rightarrow x = \dfrac{1500}{17} \approx 88$ fish.

25)

If the nth term is $an^2 + bn + c$ then

$a + b + c = 2$ $4a + 2b + c = 9$ $9a + 3b + c = 20$

     $3a + b = 7$ $5a + b = 11$

         $2a = 4$

$a = 2$
$b = 1$
$c = -1$
The nth term is $2n^2 + n - 1$.

1)

    a) $3.645 \leq x < 3.655$

    b) $2.7 \leq x < 2.8$

2)

Area $= \pi \times 15^2 = 706.85 \ldots = 707$ cm^2 correct to 3 significant figures.

3)

The next term is $10\sqrt{3} \times \frac{10\sqrt{3}}{2\sqrt{5}} = 30\sqrt{5}$

4)

Old rate $\times 1.05 = £9.03$

Old rate $= \frac{£9.03}{1.05} = £8.60$

5)

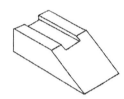

6)

$$1.05^3 \times x^4 = 1.3 \Rightarrow x^4 = \frac{1.3}{1.05^3} \Rightarrow x = \sqrt[4]{\frac{1.3}{1.05^3}} \approx 1.029$$

7)

    (1) $2x + 6y = 19 \Rightarrow 4x + 12y = 38$ (3)

    (2) $3x - 4y = 9 \quad \Rightarrow 9x - 12y = 27$ (4)

Adding equations (3) and (4) gives $13x = 65$.

$13x = 65 \Rightarrow x = \frac{65}{13} = 5$

Substituting in equation (1) $10 + 6y = 19 \Rightarrow 6y = 9 \Rightarrow y = \frac{9}{6} \Rightarrow y = \frac{3}{2}$

$x = 5$ and $y = \frac{3}{2}$

8)

$$5 \times 19 = 95$$
$$5 \times 60 = 300 \qquad\qquad 300 + 395 = 395$$
$$10 \times 14 = 140 \qquad\qquad 140 + 395 = 535$$
$$20 \times 5 = 100 \qquad\qquad 100 + 535 = 635$$

$$\frac{635}{4} = 158.75 \qquad\qquad \text{The lower quartile lies in the second interval.}$$
$$158.75 \times 3 = 476.25 \qquad\qquad \text{The upper quartile lies in the third interval.}$$

Lower quartile $= 55 + \dfrac{158.75 - 95}{300} \times 5 \approx 56.1$

Upper quartile $= 60 + \dfrac{476.25 - 395}{140} \times 10 \approx 65.8$

$$65.8 - 56.1 = 9.7$$

The interquartile range is approximately 9.7 grams.

9)

$$\frac{3x^2 - 48}{5x - 15} \div \frac{3x + 12}{25} = \frac{3(x+4)(x-4)}{5(x-3)} \times \frac{25}{3(x+4)} = \frac{5x - 20}{x - 3}$$

10)

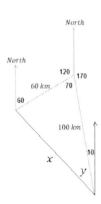

Let x be the required distance.
By the cosine rule $x^2 = 60^2 + 100^2 - 2 \times 60 \times 100 \times \cos 70°$
$x^2 \approx 9495.758..$
$x = 97.4$ km (correct to 3 significant figures)
The required bearing is $360° - y - 10°$.
By the sine rule $\dfrac{\sin y}{60} = \dfrac{\sin 70°}{97.4}$
$\sin y = \dfrac{60 \sin(70°)}{97.4} = 0.578866..$
$y = \sin^{-1} 0.578866 = 35.4°$
The bearing is $321°$.

11)

$$3x^2 - 12x + 2 = 3[x^2 - 4x] + 2 = 3[(x - 2)^2 - 4] + 2 = 3(x - 2)^2 - 10$$

12)

42.5 × 3	127.5
47.5 × 6	285
52.5 × 12	630
57.5 × 4	230
62.5 × 3	187.5
	1460

Estimated mean = $\frac{1460}{28} = 52.1$ grams.

$3 + 6 + 9 > \frac{28}{2}$.

The median lies in the interval $50 \leq m < 55$.

13)

$y \geq -2$

$y \leq x + 2$

The third line passes through (0,8) and (12,0).

This is the line with equation $2x + 3y = 24$.

The line is dotted so the required inequality is $2x + 3y < 24$.

14)

The length of the longest diagonal is $\sqrt{5^2 + 12^2 + 84^2} = 85$cm

15)

Construct a 60° angle and then bisect it.

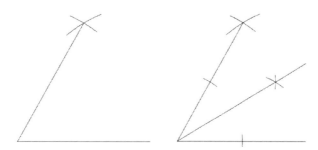

16)

Radius of Earth/radius of moon $= \frac{6371}{1737} = 3.6678..$

The volume of the moon is then the volume of the Earth ÷ $3.66678..^3$.

If the densities were the same the mass of the moon would be

the mass of the Earth ÷ $3.6678..^3 = 5.97 \times 10^{24}$ kg÷ $3.6678..^3 = 1.2099..$

The moon is less dense by a factor of $\frac{334}{552}$ so the mass of the moon is

1.2099×10^{23} kg $\times \frac{334}{552} = 7.3 \times 10^{22}$ kg, correct to two significant figures.

17)
$$x^2 - 9x - 3 = 0 \Rightarrow x^2 = 3 + 9x \Rightarrow x = \frac{3+9x}{x}$$

$x_1 = 8, \ x_2 = 9.375, \ x_3 = 9.32, \ x_4 = 9.32$

18)

9,17,25

The nth term of the sequence is $8n + 1$.

The $(n + 1)^{\text{th}}$ term is $8n + 9$.

$$(8n + 9)^2 - (8n + 1)^2 = (16n + 10)(8) = 16(8n + 5)$$

So the difference between consecutive terms is divisible by 16.

The difference between the squares of any two terms is a sum of differences between squares of consecutive terms all of which are divisible by 16 therefore the difference between the squares of any two terms is divisible by 16.

19)
$$2x^2 - 5x - 3 < 0 \Rightarrow (2x + 1)(x - 3) < 0 \Rightarrow -\frac{1}{2} < x < 3$$

20)

$6.05 \leq V < 6.15$
$1.75 \leq R < 1.85$

The upper bound of $P = \frac{6.15^2}{1.75} = 21.613$

The lower bound of $P = \frac{6.05^2}{1.85} = 19.785$

The answers agree to one significant figure but do not agree to two significant figures.

$P = 20$ correct to one significant figure.

21)

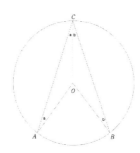

Draw the line OC. Let angle $OCA = a$ and let angle $OCB = b$.
$OC = OA = OB$ as they are all radii so triangles OCA and OCB are isosceles.
Angle OAC = angle $OAC = a$ as base angles of isosceles triangles are equal.
Similarly, angle OBC = angle $OCB = b$.
Angle $COA = 180° - 2a$ as the angles of a triangle sum to $180°$.
Similarly angle $COA = 180° - 2b$.
Angle $AOB = 360° - (180° - 2a + 180° - 2b) = 2(a + b) = 2 \times$ angle ACB.

1)

$3.6 \times 0.009 = 0.0324$

2)

$$\frac{(3x^2 \times 4x^2)^2}{6x^2} = \frac{3^2 \times 4^2 \times x^8}{6x^2} = 24x^6$$

3)

$$\frac{18.12 \times 307.64}{59.7} \approx \frac{20 \times 300}{60} = \frac{6000}{60} = 100$$

4)

(a) 6480000

(b) 0.000976

5)

$x = -\frac{9}{10}$

$x^{-1} = -\frac{10}{9}$ $\qquad x^2 = \frac{81}{100}$ $\qquad x^3 = -\frac{729}{1000}$ $\qquad x^0 = 1$

In ascending order: x^{-1} $\qquad x^3$ $\qquad x^2$ $\qquad x^0$

6)

$x = 0.6\dot{2}\dot{1}$

$10x = 6.\dot{2}\dot{1}$

$1000x = 621.\dot{2}\dot{1}$

$990x = 615$

$x = \frac{615}{990} = \frac{205}{330} = \frac{410}{660} = \frac{41}{66}$

7)

Rotation 90° clockwise about the point (5,0).

8)

$$4\frac{1}{5} \times 1\frac{2}{7} = \frac{21}{5} \times \frac{9}{7} = \frac{3}{5} \times \frac{9}{1} = \frac{27}{5} = 5\frac{2}{5}$$

9)

$$\cos 45° \times \tan 30° + \sin 45° \times \tan 60° = \frac{\sqrt{2}}{2} \times \frac{1}{\sqrt{3}} + \frac{\sqrt{2}}{2} \times \sqrt{3}$$

$$= \frac{\sqrt{2}}{2}\left(\frac{\sqrt{3}}{3} + \sqrt{3}\right) = \frac{4\sqrt{6}}{6} = \frac{2\sqrt{6}}{3}$$

10)

(a) $2x + 3y = \pi$ for example.

(b) The gradient of the given line is $-\frac{2}{3}$. The gradient of the perpendicular line is $\frac{3}{2}$.

The equation of the perpendicular line is $y = \frac{3}{2}x + c$.

$c = y - \frac{3}{2}x$

Given that the point $(-2,3)$ is on the line, $c = 3 + \frac{6}{2} = 6$.

The required equation is $y = \frac{3}{2}x + 6$

Alternatively, using the fact that $ax + by = c$ is perpendicular to $bx - ay = d$ you can write down $3x - 2y = d$ and substitute the coordinates to find $3x - 2y = -12$.

11)

$x^2 > x \Rightarrow x > 1$ or $x < 0$.

If $0 < x < 1$ then $x > x^2$.

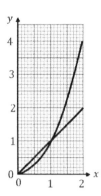

For $0 < x < 1$ the curve $y = x^2$ lies below the line $y = x$.

12)

(a) $a < b$

(b) $a = b$

(c) $a > b$

13)

$3^2 + 7^2 = 9 + 49 = 58 < 60$. The point is inside the circle.

14)

Mary paints $\frac{1}{8}$ m^2 per minute. Bob paints $\frac{1}{10}$ m^2 per minute.

Together they paint $\left(\frac{1}{8} + \frac{1}{10}\right)$ m^2 per minute $= \frac{9}{40}$ m^2 per minute.

The area to be painted is $6 \times 1.5 = 9$ m^2.

Time required $= 9 \div \frac{9}{40} = 40$ minutes.

15)

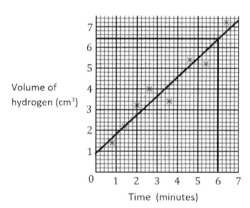

Volume of hydrogen (cm^3)

Time (minutes)

6.4 cm^3

16)

$\frac{(2x+2)(3x-4)}{x} = \frac{6x^2-2x+8}{x} = \frac{6x^2}{x} - \frac{2x}{x} + \frac{8}{x} = 6x - 2 + 8x^{-1}$

17)

$\frac{1}{1-\frac{1}{\sqrt{3}}} \times \frac{\sqrt{3}}{\sqrt{3}} = \frac{\sqrt{3}}{\sqrt{3}-1} \times \frac{\sqrt{3}+1}{\sqrt{3}+1} = \frac{3+\sqrt{3}}{2}$

18)

$$\text{Area} = \frac{1}{2} \times 6 \times 6 \times \sin 60 = 18 \times \frac{\sqrt{3}}{2} = 9\sqrt{3}.$$

19)

Height, h (metres)	Frequency	Cumulative Frequency
$1.5 \leq h < 1.6$	3	3
$1.6 \leq h < 1.7$	5	8
$1.7 \leq h < 1.8$	12	20
$1.8 \leq h < 1.9$	10	30
$1.9 \leq h < 2.0$	2	32

(a)

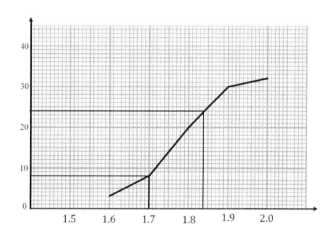

(b) Upper quartile $= 1.84$. Lower quartile $= 1.7$.

Interquartile range $= 1.84 - 1.7 = 0.14$ m.

(c) $\frac{8}{32} = \frac{1}{4}$

20)

$$\frac{1}{x} = x - \frac{8}{x} \Rightarrow 1 = x^2 - 8 \Rightarrow x^2 = 9 \Rightarrow x = 3 \text{ or } x = -3$$

21)

If the nth term is $an^2 + bn + c$ then

$a + b + c = 4$ $\qquad\qquad$ $4a + 2b + c = 12$ $\qquad\qquad$ $9a + 3c + c = 24$

$\qquad 3a + b = 8$ $\qquad\qquad\qquad$ $5a + b = 12$

$\qquad\qquad 2a = 4$

$a = 2$
$b = 2$
$c = 0$

The nth term is $2n^2 + 2n$.

22)

$$\frac{6x^2 - 3x - 3}{12x^2 + 14x + 4} = \frac{(3x-3)(2x+1)}{2(3x+2)(2x+1)} = \frac{3x-3}{3x+2}$$

23)

$$\cos BAC = \frac{5^2 + 8^2 - 7^2}{2 \times 5 \times 8} = \frac{40}{80} = \frac{1}{2}$$

$\cos 60° = \frac{1}{2}$ therefore angle $BAC = 60°$

24)

$$x^2 + y^2 = 10$$
$$x + 2y = 5$$

$x = 5 - 2y \Rightarrow x^2 = (5 - 2y)^2 = 4y^2 - 20y + 25$
$4y^2 - 20y + 25 + y^2 = 10 \Rightarrow 5y^2 - 20y + 15 = 0 \Rightarrow y^2 - 4y + 3 = 0$
$\Rightarrow (y - 1)(y - 3) = 0 \Rightarrow y = 1$ or $y = 3$.
If $y = 1$ then $x = 5 - 2 = 3$.
If $y = 3$ then $x = 5 - 6 = -1$.

$x = 3$ and $y = 1$ or $x = -1$ and $y = 3$

25)

$f(2) = 1$
$ff(2) = f(1) = 2$
$fff(2) = f(2) = 1$
$ffff(2) = f(1) = 2$
$fffff(2) = f(2) = 1$

1)
$$\frac{\sqrt{2.3^3+1.1\times9.3}+4.6}{2.07^3\times4.871} = 0.2160085862$$

2)

The first six terms are

$$2 \qquad 2+x \qquad 4+x \quad 6+2x \quad 10+3x \qquad 16+5x$$
$$16+5x = 41 \Rightarrow 5x = 25 \Rightarrow x = 5$$
The third term is $4 + 5 = 9$

3)

$$\cos ABC = \frac{6}{7}$$
$$ABC = \cos^{-1}\left(\frac{6}{7}\right) = 31°$$

4)

$$x = \frac{9 \pm \sqrt{9^2 - 4 \times 1 \times -7}}{2 \times 1} = \frac{9 \pm \sqrt{109}}{2}$$
$$x = 9.72 \text{ or } x = -0.72$$

5)

The diameter of the ball is 23cm.

$$\frac{100}{23} > 4 \qquad \frac{70}{23} > 3 \qquad \frac{50}{23} > 2$$

It is possible to fit $4 \times 3 \times 2 = 24$ balls in the box.

The volume of the box is $100 \times 70 \times 50 = 350000$ cm³.

The volume of a ball is $\frac{4}{3} \times \pi \times 11.5^3 = 6370.626$ cm³.

$\frac{350000}{6370.626} \approx 54.9 < 55$ therefore it is not possible to fit 55 balls in the box.

6)
$$(2x + 3)(3x - 2) - 4(x - 5) = 6x^2 + 5x - 6 - 4x + 20 = 6x^2 + x + 14$$

7)

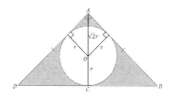

Let $BD = 2x.$ $AC = x.$ $\qquad x^2 = 8 \Rightarrow x = 2\sqrt{2}$

$$r + \sqrt{2}r = 2\sqrt{2} \Rightarrow r(1 + \sqrt{2}) = 2\sqrt{2} \Rightarrow r = \frac{2\sqrt{2}}{1+\sqrt{2}} = 4 - 2\sqrt{2}$$

$r^2 = 24 - 16\sqrt{2}.$ $\qquad$ The area of the circle is $\pi(24 - 16\sqrt{2})$ cm².

The shaded area is $\left(8 - \pi(24 - 16\sqrt{2})\right)$cm² ≈ 3.69 cm².

8)

$$f(x)g(x) = 20 \Rightarrow (x+3)(x-5) = 20$$
$$\Rightarrow x^2 - 2x - 15 = 20 \Rightarrow x^2 - 2x - 35 = 0$$
$$\Rightarrow (x-7)(x+5) = 0 \Rightarrow x = 7 \text{ or } x = -5.$$

9)

$$y = ax + bx \Rightarrow y = x(a+b) \Rightarrow x = \frac{y}{a+b}$$

10)

$$4x - 2y = 7 \qquad (1)$$
$$6x + 6y = 24 \qquad (2)$$

Multiply (1) by 3 to get
$$12x - 6y = 21 \qquad (3)$$
Add equations (2) and (3)
$$18x = 45 \Rightarrow x = \frac{45}{18} = 2.5$$
Substitute in (1)
$$4(2.5) - 2y = 7 \Rightarrow -2y = 7 - 10 \Rightarrow y = 1.5$$
$$x = 2.5 \text{ and } y = 1.5$$

11)

Time (t seconds)	Frequency	Frequency density
$9.9 \le t < 10.1$	3	15
$10.1 \le t < 10.3$	6	30
$10.3 \le t < 10.35$	9	180
$10.35 \le t < 10.4$	4	80
$10.4 \le t < 10.6$	2	10

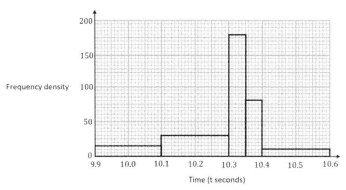

Number of athletes with times below 10.2 s $\approx 3 + \frac{6}{2} = 6$

12)

$$3(x-5) = 6(2x+4) \Rightarrow 3x - 15 = 12x + 24 \Rightarrow -39 = 9x \Rightarrow x = -\frac{39}{9} = -\frac{13}{3}$$

13)

Volume of ice = 600 cm^3.
Mass of ice = $600 \times 0.92 = 552$g
Mass of water = 552 g.
Volume of water = 552 cm^3.
Area of base of cylinder = $\pi \times 7.5^2$ cm^2= 176.714 cm^2.
Depth $= \frac{552}{176.714} = 3.1$cm.

14)

If the difference between each term and the previous term is d then the first four
terms are 7 $7 + d$ $7 + 2d$ and $7 + 3d$.
The sum of these terms is $28 + 6d$.
$28 + 6d = 37 \Rightarrow 6d = 9 \Rightarrow d = 1.5$
The first two terms are 7 and 8.5.
The nth term is $1.5n + 5.5$

15)

7,13,19
The nth term of the sequence is $6n + 1$.
The $(n + 1)^{\text{th}}$ term is $6n + 7$

$$(6n + 7)^2 - (6n + 1)^2 = (12n + 8)(6) = 24(3n + 2)$$

So the difference between consecutive terms is divisible by 24.

The difference between the squares of any two terms is a sum of differences between
squares of consecutive terms all of which are divisible by 24 therefore the difference
between the squares of any two terms is divisible by 24.

16)

Let the two cubes be $(n + 1)^3$ and n^3.
The difference is $(n + 1)^3 - n^3$.

$(n + 1)^3 - n^3 = 22447 \Rightarrow$
$(n + 1)(n^2 + 2n + 1) - n^3 = 22447 \Rightarrow$
$n^3 + 3n^2 + 3n + 1 - n^3 = 22447 \Rightarrow$
$3n^2 + 3n - 22446 = 0 \Rightarrow$
$n^2 + n - 7482 = 0 \Rightarrow$
$(n + 87)(n - 86) = 0 \Rightarrow$
$n = 86$
The cubes are $86^3 = 636056$ and $87^3 = 658503$.

17)

Amy, Bob and Carol share some money in the ratio 7:5:4. Between them Amy and Carol
receive £180 more than Bob. How much does Bob get?

$$\frac{7 + 4 - 5}{7 + 5 + 4} = \frac{6}{16}$$

$\frac{6}{16} \times \text{total} = 180.$

Bob receives $\frac{5}{16} \times \text{total} = \frac{5}{6} \times 180 = £150.$

18)

$2000 \times m^4 = 2251.05 \Rightarrow m^4 = \frac{2251.05}{2000} \Rightarrow m = \left(\frac{2251.05}{2000}\right)^{\frac{1}{4}} = 1.03 = 103\%$
The interest rate was 3%.

19)

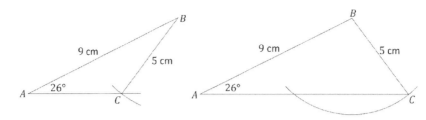

$\frac{\sin C}{9} = \frac{\sin 26°}{5} \Rightarrow \sin C = \frac{9 \sin 26°}{5} = 0.7890..$

$C = \sin^{-1} \left(\frac{9 \sin 26°}{5} \right) = 51.1°$ as shown in the second diagram.

$180° - 51.1° = 127.9°.$

The two possible values for angle BCA are $51.1°$ and $127.9°$.

20)

The diameter is 4 cm. The area of the square is $4 \times 4 = 16$ cm^2.

21)

$\overrightarrow{BA} = \boldsymbol{a} - \boldsymbol{b}$

$\frac{BP}{BA} = \frac{y}{x+y}$

$\overrightarrow{BP} = \frac{y}{x+y}(\boldsymbol{a} - \boldsymbol{b})$

$\overrightarrow{OP} = \overrightarrow{OB} + \overrightarrow{BP} = b + \frac{y}{x+y}(\boldsymbol{a} - \boldsymbol{b}) = \frac{(x+y)b+y(a-b)}{x+y} = \frac{xb+ya}{x+y}$

1)

Area $= \frac{1}{2}(4+5) \times 2 = 9$ units

Perimeter $= 4 + 5 + \sqrt{2^2 + 2^2} + \sqrt{1^2 + 2^2} = 14.06$ units².

2)

$\frac{1}{4^{-2}} = 4^2 = 16$

$(6x^3 y^2)^0 = 1$

3)

$(4x - 3)(2x + 5) = 8x^2 + 14x - 15$

4)

$\frac{12x^3 y}{2xy^4} = 6x^2 y^{-3}$ or $\frac{6x^2}{y^3}$

5)

The gradient of the line with equation $ax + by = c$ is $-\frac{a}{b}$.

The gradient of the line with equation $bx - ay = d$ is $\frac{b}{a}$.

The product of the gradients is $-\frac{a}{b} \times \frac{b}{a} = -1$.

The product of the gradients is -1 therefore the lines are perpendicular.

6)

$(3n + 1)^2 - (3n + 1) = 9n^2 + 6n + 1 - 3n - 1 = 9n^2 + 3n = 3(3n^2 + n)$.

Since $3n^2 + n$ is a positive integer for all positive integer values of n,

$3(3n^2 + n)$ is a multiple of 3 for all positive integer values of n

7)

$2 + \sqrt{3} + 2 - \sqrt{3} = 4$

$(2 + \sqrt{3})(2 - \sqrt{3}) = 1$

$\frac{2+\sqrt{3}}{2-\sqrt{3}} = \frac{2+\sqrt{3}}{2-\sqrt{3}} \times \frac{2+\sqrt{3}}{2+\sqrt{3}} = 7 + 4\sqrt{(3)}$

8)

$x(ax + bx - ay - by) = x\big(x(a + b) - y(a + b)\big) = x(a + b)(x - y)$

9)

$2 - \frac{2x}{x+2} = \frac{2(x+2)}{x+2} - \frac{2x}{x+2} = \frac{2x+4-2x}{x+2} = \frac{4}{x+2}$

$\frac{2}{x+4} + \frac{2}{x^2+7x+12} = \frac{2}{x+4} + \frac{2}{(x+3)(x+4)} = \frac{2(x+3)}{(x+3)(x+4)} + \frac{2}{(x+3)(x+4)}$

$= \frac{2x+6+2}{(x+3)(x+4)} = \frac{2x+8}{(x+3)(x+4)} = \frac{2(x+4)}{(x+3)(x+4)} = \frac{2}{x+3}$

10)

$x^3 + 2x - 26 = 0 \Rightarrow x^3 = 26 - 2x \Rightarrow x = \sqrt[3]{26 - 2x}$

$x_0 = 3 \Rightarrow x_1 = 2.714 \Rightarrow x_2 = 2.740 \Rightarrow x_3 = 2.738 \Rightarrow x = 2.738$

$x = 2.738$ correct to 3 decimal places.

11)
$$45 \times 225 = 3^2 \times 5 \times 3^2 \times 5^2 = 3^4 \times 5^3$$
$$a = 4$$

12)
$$9x^2 - 1 = (3x + 1)(3x - 1)$$
$$9x^4 - 1 = (3x^2 + 1)(3x^2 - 1)$$

13)

The diagram shows an equilateral triangle with sides of length 2.

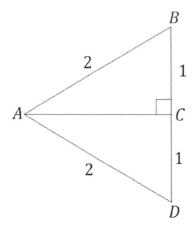

AC bisects angle BAD and is perpendicular to BD.
Angle BAC is therefore $30°$. By Pythagoras' theorem $AC^2 = 2^2 - 1^2 = 3$.
$AC = \sqrt{3}$.
$$\cos BAC = \frac{AC}{AB}$$
$$\cos 30° = \frac{\sqrt{3}}{2}$$

14)
$$3x^2 - 8x + 4 = (3x - 2)(x - 2)$$

$$3x^2 - 8x + 4 = 0 \Rightarrow (3x - 2)(x - 2) = 0 \Rightarrow x = \frac{2}{3} \text{ or } x = 2$$

15)
$$k = \frac{m(2+x)}{7-x} \Rightarrow k(7 - x) = m(2 + x) \Rightarrow 7k - 7x = 2m + mx \Rightarrow$$
$$7k - 2m = mx + 7x \Rightarrow 7k - 2m = x(m + 7) \Rightarrow x = \frac{7k-2m}{m+7}$$

16)

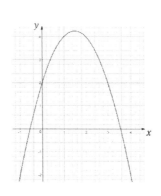

17)
$$g(x + 1) = (x + 1)^2 + 1 = x^2 + 2x + 2$$
$$gf(x) = g(x - 3) = (x - 3)^2 + 1 = x^2 - 6x + 10$$
$$f^{-1}(x) = x + 3 \qquad f^{-1}(3) = 6$$

18)

At the points where the lines cross the x axis, the y coordinate is 0.

On the line with equation $x + 2y = 10$, when $y = 0$, $x = 10$.

On the line with equation $y = x + 2$, when $y = 0$, $x = -2$.

Where the lines intersect $x + 2(x + 2) = 10 \Rightarrow 3x + 4 = 10 \Rightarrow$

$3x = 6 \Rightarrow x = 6$ and $y = 4$.

The base of the triangle is 12 units and the height is 4 units.

The area of the triangle is $\frac{12 \times 4}{2} = 24$ units^2.

19)
$$c = \frac{4.53 \times 10^{87}}{(2.76 \times 10^{-37})^2} = \frac{4.53}{2.76^2} \times \frac{10^{87}}{10^{-74}} = 0.595 \times 10^{161} = 5.95 \times 10^{160}$$

20)

The probability of taking a red bead followed by a blue bead is $\frac{n}{n+7} \times \frac{7}{n+6}$.

This is the same as the probability of taking a blue bead followed by a red bead.

Therefore $\frac{n}{n+7} \times \frac{7}{n+6} = \frac{4}{15}$

$$\frac{7n}{(n+7)(n+6)} = \frac{4}{15} \Rightarrow 105n = 4(n + 7)(n + 6) \Rightarrow$$

$$4(n^2 + 13n + 42) = 105n \Rightarrow 4n^2 + 52n - 105n + 168 = 0 \Rightarrow$$

$$4n^2 - 53n + 168 = 0$$

$$4n^2 - 53n + 168 = 0 \Rightarrow (4n - 21)(n - 8) = 0 \Rightarrow n = 8 \text{ or } n = \frac{21}{4}$$

There 8 red beads and 15 beads in total.

The probability of taking two blue beads is $\frac{7}{15} \times \frac{6}{14} = \frac{1}{5}$

Printed in Great Britain
by Amazon